D1605998

A Confusion
of Printers

Wycliffe Studies in History,
Church, and Society

GENERAL EDITOR: THOMAS P. POWER

The series aims to draw on historical scholarship from new and established scholars in the
history of Christianity broadly defined. Titles
in the series will be topical but general enough
to be appealing. The subject matter will cover
topics of general interest in the field of Christian history. The goal is to produce short pamphlets on historical topics of broad general
interest in an accessible way.

A Confusion
of Printers

*The Role of Print in the
English Reformation*

BY
Pearce J. Carefoote

WIPF & STOCK · Eugene, Oregon

A CONFUSION OF PRINTERS
The Role of Print in the English Reformation

Wipf & Stock
An Imprint of Wipf and Stock Publishers
199 W. 8th Ave., Suite 3
Eugene, OR 97401

www.wipfandstock.com

PAPERBACK ISBN: 978-1-7252-5214-1
HARDCOVER ISBN: 978-1-7252-5215-8
EBOOK ISBN: 978-1-7252-5216-5

Manufactured in the U.S.A.   OCTOBER 15, 2019

Contents

List of Figures

Permission for the reproduction of images was granted by the following institutions:

The Thomas Fisher Rare Book Library, University of Toronto Library (figures 1, 4, 5–10); the Beinecke Rare Book and Manuscript Library, Yale University (figure 2); and the Library of the Pontifical Institute of Medieval Studies, Toronto (figure 3).

Introduction

FEW THINGS REPRESENT THE whimsical cleverness of the English language as well as its collective nouns: a murder of crows, a pride of lions, a murmur of nuns, a fleet of printers. This last collective noun was almost certainly chosen in tacit acknowledgment of the important role played by London's Fleet Street, the famous street on which, until very recently, English printers and publishers operated for centuries. When Reuters finally left central London in 2003, with it went five hundred years of tumultuous history on the narrow road that once was known as "the street of adventure." However, since so many of our collective nouns have their origins in the late Middle Ages, I wonder whether, in that turbulent period when England was transitioning from the medieval to the modern era, when, in the period we now call the Reformation, Wynkyn de Worde (1455–1534) and his colleagues were setting up shop on Fleet Street, it would not have been better to refer to them and their successors as a "confusion of printers" instead.

A confusion of printers. The social history of the Reformation era remains a constant source of fascination for scholars. A major area of focus is the ways in which the movement intersected with print to help give birth to what we today call the modern era. One consistent theme is that while the story of the Reformation cannot be told without reference to the books, pamphlets, broadsides, and engravings that helped to spread it, oftentimes the more interesting stories are to be found in the trials and tribulations of the printers themselves. The Reformation (or, perhaps more correctly, the Reformations) of the sixteenth century was, among other things, about courageous printers, deeply committed printers, displaced printers, refugee printers, and, at times, cold, calculating printers who just wanted to make a profit. Without them, the message of the Reformation and the Catholic Reformation would have been so seriously limited that it is hard to imagine the movement that changed the Western world forever gaining the remarkable traction that it did. But the uncertainties associated with being a printer or publisher in that unsettled period between 1517 and 1648, the year when the wars of religion finally came to a close, cannot be underestimated. And nowhere was it more uncertain and confusing than it was in England. As it turned out, however, that turbulence helped set the stage for the achievement of the freedom of the press by the end of the seventeenth century, a feat that had been unthinkable when the Tudors occupied the throne.

1

Origins

THE ROOTS OF THAT uniquely English confusion are not to be found in the actions of a lone German friar affixing his *Theses* to a chapel door in 1517. Neither are they to be found in the effects of Luther's teaching, which, thanks to the magical swiftness of the printing press, reached and was debated in Cambridge as early as 1518. It is certainly true that the introduction of Lutheran ideas led to controversy and confusion in England; the bishop of London, Cuthbert Tunstall (1474–1559), commanded the booksellers of the city not to import books without an episcopal license, and no books could be printed in England without the permission of a board of censors that included Tunstall, Cardinal Thomas Wolsey (1473–1530), and Bishop John Fisher (ca. 1469–1535), but the law was regularly flouted.[1] Furthermore, Henry VIII's formal separation from the Church of Rome in 1534 did not, in the end, alter his official condemnation of Lutheranism one iota, serving to make the religious and political environment in England even murkier.

1. Gilmont, *Reformation*, 266–67.

Even so, none of these realities was the original source of the confusion—not to mention dangers—in which the scribes and printers and booksellers of England had to operate, especially for the first few decades of the Reformation era. To find that source, we must look back one century earlier, to the time of the proto-Protestant John Wycliffe (1330–1384) and his followers, the Lollards, and to a document known as the *Constitutions of Oxford* of 1408, issued by the archbishop of Canterbury, Thomas Arundel (1353–1414).[2]

According to Arundel's decree the possession of even a scrap of the Bible in English translation was sufficient to warrant the proffering of charges. This was intended to counter the perceived effects of an unauthorized English translation of the Bible done by Wycliffe and his followers around the turn of the fifteenth century that was then circulating around the country. The seventh clause of the *Constitutions* explicitly forbade the translation of any part of the Bible into English, with anyone violating the clause subject to excommunication and a charge of heresy—not something to be toyed with at the end of the Middle Ages. To make matters even more complicated, Arundel's *Constitutions* were generally combined with King Henry IV's 1401 edict *De heretico comburendo* (On the burning of heretics), according to which those found guilty of such an offence as translating

2. Daniell, *William Tyndale*, 57.

even a small portion of the Scriptures into the vulgar tongue were liable to be burned alive.[3]

Contemporaries, however, were rather uncertain about how to implement that ban. In 1529, Sir Thomas More (1478–1535), for example, claimed that the ban applied only to Wycliffe's translation and that non-Wycliffite vernacular versions could be legally owned by ordinary Englishmen.[4] Unfortunately for those who wanted to read Scripture in their native tongue, there were no large-scale English translation projects aside from the forbidden ones undertaken by the Lollards a century earlier. More's exemption, however, might help explain how vernacular translations of the Old Testament done by William Caxton (1422–1491) at the end of the fifteenth century, and found in his printings of *The Golden Legend*, for example, may not have led to his condemnation. Whatever the case, Wycliffite manuscript copies of the English Bible found places in the homes of otherwise law-abiding Catholics and were assumed to be Catholic. Surviving wills from the period record wealthy benefactors publicly bequeathing "my English Bible" to members of the clergy.[5] About two-hundred fifty Wycliffe Bible manuscripts still survive, and their large physical size certainly suggests that they were intended for use in church. Wycliffite Bibles were found in religious houses as well as in the libraries of all the kings who

3. Killick, "Treason, Felony, and Lollardy," 240.

4. Marshall, *Heretics and Believers*, 118.

5. Marshall, *Heretics and Believers*, 118.

fought in the Wars of the Roses.[6] Quite clearly, then, the rich had access to the divine word in their own language—so why not ordinary subjects? The simple answer is that Arundel's *Constitutions* still remained in force in Henry VIII's England. It was against this backdrop that English printers plied their trade as the Reformation began to unfold. The fact that by the 1530s there was open access to the vernacular Scriptures in every other European country except England must have been a source of confusion and frustration.

6. Marshall, *Heretics and Believers*, 119.

2

The Bible of William Tyndale

THE TEST CASE FOR this would be William Tyndale
(1494–1536), who would loom large over the fraught
print history of the early English Bible. Tyndale, a
priest from the area around Gloucester, where the
Lollards had had a strong presence, firmly believed
that people possessed the right to read the Scriptures
in their own language—not just the aristocrats or
members of the court but even the boy who pulled
the plough. His first translation, which enriched
the English language with such memorable phrases
as "flowing with milk and honey" and "signs of the
times," was begun in Cologne in 1525, as far removed
as possible from the reaches of English law. Owing
to civil and religious unrest in that city, however, the
project was interrupted numerous times, so it was not
until 1526 that his translation was finished, with the
first octavo copies printed at Worms, while a second,
pirated edition was issued at Antwerp in a smaller
format by Christoffel van Ruremund (d. 1531) later
that same year.[1] Tyndale's New Testament represents

1. Blayney, *Stationers' Company*, 229.

the first book explicitly intended to serve an English Protestant audience, such as it was at the time. Copies rapidly made their way across the channel and soon appeared on the London market, rattling Henry's court. The book was, of course, illegal, but the greatest problem, according to Bishop Tunstall, was the "inter meddling there with many heretical articles and erroneous opinions,"[2] an acknowledgment of the fact that Tyndale's prologues to the Pauline Epistles were based on Luther's.

According to Tunstall's decree issued on 23 October 1526, all copies of Tyndale's New Testament were to be surrendered within thirty days. That, however, did not stop the Continental printers from issuing ten more editions over the next decade, infuriating King Henry, his chancellor Thomas More, and members of the episcopacy. It also did not prevent booksellers from importing it. It is known, for example, that in 1528 a Dutchman by the name of John Raymund was disciplined for bringing five hundred copies into the country, importation laws notwithstanding.[3] The archbishop of Canterbury even began a campaign to purchase Tyndale's Testaments on the Continent wherever he could find them and subsequently commit them to the flames, much to the delight of Tyndale and his printers. By buying up the contraband, the bishops of England were financing the next editions that would be printed.[4] To give a sense of the expense

2. Daniell, *William Tyndale*, 190.

3. Blayney, *Stationers' Company*, 250.

4. Blayney, *Stationers' Company*, 250–51.

versus the profitability of producing Tyndale's New Testament, it is estimated that they were printed in runs of five thousand copies per edition, with each volume selling for two shillings two pence each. Since most unskilled workers made about four pence a day, that would mean it cost the average laborer four and a half days' wages to buy a copy, making acquisition difficult but not impossible.[5]

The edition of 1534, printed at Antwerp by Martin de Keyser, survives in greatest numbers and marks Tyndale's final revision of his earlier work.

5. Pardue, *Printing*, 82.

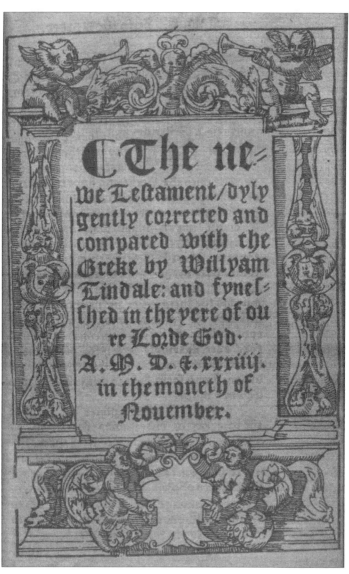

Title page to the Tyndale New Testament, printed at
Antwerp in 1534.

Together with the other Reformers of his day, Tyndale believed that the Bible had to be translated into the people's language not only for their comprehension but also in order to release the text from the allegorical interpretations that had become so common in the medieval church. Tyndale recorded his objections to the scholastic treatment of Scripture in his preface to this edition, boldly writing that

> the kyngdome of heaven which is the Scripture and worde of God maybe so locked up that he which readeth or heareth it cannot understonde it; as Christ testifieth how that the Scribes and Pharises had to shut it up . . . that their Jewes which thought themselves within were yet so locked out and are to this daye that they can understande no sentence of the scripture unto their salvacion though they can reherse the textes everywhere and dispute thereof as sottelye as ye popysh doctoures of dunces darcke learnynge which with their sophistrye sarved us as ye Pharises did the Jewes.[6]

In 1535, Tyndale was arrested in Antwerp, where he was working on a translation of the Hebrew Scriptures. He was then taken to Brussels and in the following year was strangled and burned at the stake, with copies of his books reportedly serving as the tinder. Although all vernacular translations were initially opposed by the English Church, no version since Wycliffe's was as violently suppressed as was Tyndale's New Testament; but given the popularity and economic success of the volume, what were

---

6. *The Newe Testament* (1534), ii.

English printers and booksellers to do in order to meet the obvious demand?

The simple answer was to plagiarize Tyndale's work. Henry remained suspicious of vernacular Bibles even after his break with Rome, and Tyndale's rendering, despite its erudition and poetry, represented a bridge too far for him. That was due in part to the Protestant influence behind the ways in which Tyndale had chosen to translate certain words, preferring "congregation" over "church" and "elder" over "priest," for example. Tyndale's truly unforgiveable sin, however, was his defiance and disregard of royal authority in the matter. (Criticizing Henry's divorce from Catherine of Aragon did not help his case either.) So when Henry finally gave permission for an authorized translation of the Scriptures to appear in 1539, the editors and printers turned to what they had readily at hand: Tyndale.

3

Bibles after Tyndale

THE RESULT WAS THE so-called Great Bible, an approved version of the English Scriptures reflecting Henry's quite conservative tastes. In effect, it was a recension and revision of Tyndale's original translation. The printing of the first edition was actually begun in France, owing in part to the perception that French printing houses still possessed greater skill, combined with the fact that no English printer yet operated a press large enough for the required paper size. The decision to print on the Continent also coincided with the reality that there were many conservatives in England, especially among the bishops, who were sufficiently opposed to the venture that they would have happily disrupted its due course at home. Work on the project was brought to a halt in Paris when the French inquisitor general issued an order against corrupt Bible translations, with the original French printer, François Regnault, personally cited by the authorities. Myles Coverdale (1488–1569), who was Tyndale's friend and the editor of the Great Bible, together with the publishers, Edward Whitchurch (d.

1561) and Richard Grafton (d. 1573), left for London, having shipped almost eight tons of recently printed sheets ahead of them, while about five tons were left behind in France. The Englishmen also purchased some of Regnault's equipment in order to continue the work back in London and managed to retrieve marked-up printer's copy for the confiscated sheets as well as those not yet printed.

No credit was given to Tyndale's scholarship in the massive tome. Nevertheless, his words survived in the Great Bible, as well as in its immediate predecessor, the Matthew Bible, printed at Antwerp by Whitchurch and Grafton in 1537. Interestingly, in the latter Bible an *hommage* to Tyndale—his ornamental initials hidden by the printers in plain sight at the end of the book of the prophet Malachi—can still be found. That page was most certainly not shown to the king when the book was presented to him by his chancellor, Thomas Cromwell (1485–1540), and his archbishop of Canterbury, Thomas Cranmer (1489–1556), as a possible model for future domestic English Bible production. More importantly, Tyndale's words survive in its successors the Geneva, the Bishops', and ultimately the King James Bibles. Indeed, it is estimated that nine-tenths of the "Authorized" Version is actually the work of Tyndale, the man printers could steal from but acknowledged at their peril.[1] Publishing Tyndale is but one example of the challenges faced by printers at the beginning of the Reformation in England. By the end of Henry's

---

1. Lewis, *English Bible from KJV to NIV*, 22.

reign, as he swung into and out of the Reformed camp with increasingly regularity, the guiding principle for printers and booksellers was certainly not the Lutheran as could be found in Saxony, or the Reformed as found in Geneva, or the Catholic in Rome. In those places the cause of maintaining tradition or embracing reform had achieved critical mass within the general population. Such was not yet the case in Henry's England, where the monarch's changeability translated into uncertainty, instability, and danger for authors, printers, and the public alike.

4

The King and Printers

RICHARD GRAFTON, THE OFFICIAL king's printer, is a case in point. He had been responsible for the publication of some of the hallmarks of early English Reformation literature, including the Matthew Bible of 1537, the Great Bible of 1539, and the *Primer* of 1540. He may have thought that the path of reform was moving unrelentingly toward his desired Protestant goal, but he was very much mistaken in this sense of security. Although he was the king's printer, he was nevertheless imprisoned in the Tower of London in 1541 for possessing a pamphlet by Philip Melanchthon that criticized Henry's Six Articles of 1539, the issuing of which had caused the Church of England to tack once again toward a more Catholic sensibility. Then, in 1543, he and his partner Edward Whitchurch and six others were imprisoned for printing unlawful religious books. It must also have confused and disappointed him that access to the Great Bible, Grafton's masterpiece, had become legally restricted to certain classes of people, excluding nine-tenths of the general population by the time of Henry's death. The conservative atmosphere that pervaded Henry's court ensured that the Great Bible would not be printed again until 1549, three years into the reign of the boy king, Edward VI (1537–1553).

In another case of mixed messages, the theologically conservative Henry appointed men from the Reformed camp to serve as tutors to his son. As a result, there must have been some sense of relief, perhaps even exultation, among the Protestant printers and stationers of the kingdom when the nine-year-old Edward VI ascended the throne in January of 1547. Under the protection of his uncle, Edward Seymour, they must have hoped for the reform of the censorship laws that still seemed so draconian more than a decade after the split from Rome. Their hopes were initially rewarded. Toward the end of the first year of his reign, Edward's parliament repealed all acts concerning treason passed since 1377 that in any way touched on matters of religion.[1] This now meant that the English Scriptures and other texts by the Continental Reformers could be legally printed in England. As Peter Blayney details in his masterful history of the Stationers' Company, the number of printers increased from twenty-seven under Henry VIII to thirty-four under his son Edward.[2] Edward also initially sent a strong signal of liberality by dismissing his father's rather conservative printer, Thomas Berthelet (d. 1555), only three months after ascending the throne, and replacing him with

1. Blayney, *Stationers' Company*, 602.

2. Blayney, *Stationers' Company*, 604–5.

Richard Grafton, late of the Tower of London. Protestant refugee printers and stationers such as Stephen Mierdman (d. 1559), Walter Lynne (d. 1571), Thomas Gualthier, and quite possibly Egidius van der Erve, to name but four, began leaving their persecuted homes on the Continent for London, where it appeared that they could practice both their faith and the trade in peace. The result was an explosion of printing. While in the early 1540s London presses produced about one hundred editions of books annually, that number rose to 192 by 1547. The following year saw 268 new publications, the vast majority of which were religious in character, including Bibles, catechisms, and pamphlets attacking the Roman church and its customs and beliefs.[3]

The road to change, however, is rarely a straight one, and the brief, transitional reign of Edward VI was no different in that regard. The very first Edwardian parliament, which assembled in November of 1547 to abrogate many of the censorship laws, sent mixed signals as well. On the one hand, it declared that all images were to be removed from the churches, one of the hallmarks of a Genevan-style reform. On the other, that same parliament, as its very first act, ordered the punishment of anyone who published material that spoke contemptuously of the sacrament of the altar.[4] Quite obviously, the theological wars over the nature of Christ's presence in the Eucharist remained a vital point of contention within the English Church at this

3. Marshall, *Heretics and Believers*, 315.
4. Blayney, *Stationers' Company*, 604.

stage, with some advocating for a more traditional Catholic or Lutheran explanation, while others assumed a more radical Zwinglian position that saw it simply as a memorial. It would remain a moot point in Edward's first *Book of Common Prayer*, published in 1549. But clearly printers were given some latitude in publications about certain theological topics but not others.

If Protestant printers enjoyed some halcyon days for a while, they were not to last. In 1548 two particular publications that were especially offensive to Catholics appeared in the stationers' shops, mocking the Mass: *An Indictment against Mother Mass* and *A Brief Recantation of Mistress Missa*, in which the consecrated host was referred to as a "Jack in the box", an act of blasphemy in the eyes of many.

John Day (d. 1584), the man who would go on to print Foxe's *Book of Martyrs* during Queen Elizabeth's reign, in that year printed Luke Shepherd's poem *John Bon and the Mast Person*, a particularly acerbic attack on traditional eucharistic doctrine and piety. Some prominent Catholics in London demanded that the lord mayor seize the printer and keep him in custody until he provided the author's name.[5] Day managed to escape. When a Catholic London hosier named Miles Huggard responded to these bits of Protestant doggerel with his pamphlet *Answer to the Ballad Called Abuse of ye Blessed Sacrament*, his publication was suppressed, and he was forced to appear before

5. Evenden and Freeman, *Religion*, 13.

the council.[6] These were confusing times indeed for advocates on both sides of the theological debate.

These small but enlightening vignettes provide some sense of the undecided character and dogmatic instability that remained a mark of the Church of England more than a decade after its formal separation from Rome. In response to these theological skirmishes, provoked in no small way by printers on both sides of the religious divide, the Privy Council began to exercise greater control over a press that was clearly not taking Parliament's instructions seriously enough. For the first time, literary licensing would be placed in the hands of civil rather than religious authorities.[7] This change, however, did not really alter the climate in which printers and booksellers operated. In an era when the printing of radical religious and political propaganda was being actively encouraged by some, conservative elements in society still had the ability to retaliate. For printers, therefore, it was difficult to determine who among "the powers that be" (as Tyndale so elegantly phrased it in Romans 13:1) was to be trusted. Clarity about law and practice surrounding religious publication was still only a dream. That clarity was eventually achieved, though not in the way that the Protestant stationers of London would have preferred, when on 28 April 1551 Edward issued a new proclamation against unlawful printing. The young king, we are told, was "most sorry and earnestly from the bottom of his heart doth

6. Marshall, *Heretics and Believers*, 316.

7. Blayney, *Stationers' Company*, 738.

lament to hear and see many of his subjects to abuse daily by their vicious living and corrupt conversation that most precious jewel, the word of God."[8] From that point on, Edward's regulations would be far harsher than his father's. Royal permission or the permission of six Privy Counsellors would now be required before a license to print would be granted; and not only printers who violated this law, but also those private persons found to be in possession of contraband literature, would be punished.[9] And so the situation remained until young Edward died in July of 1553 at the age of sixteen, succeeded by his Catholic half-sister Mary I (1516–1558).

8. Gilmont, *Reformation*, 284.
9. Blayney, *Stationers' Company*, 742.

5

Change under Mary

THERE SHOULD BE NO surprise that the change of regime meant significant change for printers, publishers, and booksellers. At the time of Edward VI's death in July of 1553, there were seventeen presses active in London; two months into the reign of his successor, Mary, only eight were left in operation, as Protestant printers either fled to the relative safety of the Continent or simply closed shop. This statistic, however, is slightly misleading. For one thing, a number of the refugee Protestant printers had already returned home in the last year of Edward's reign as restrictions on print were tightened. The fact is that, under Mary, the state of printing and publishing books in England effectively returned to what it had been during her father's reign, if not somewhat improved. Under Henry, there were forty-nine stationers, of whom twenty-seven were printers. During Mary's reign there were fifty-two stationers, of whom twenty-seven were printers. For the first half of the sixteenth century, therefore, the situation in Henry's and Mary's reigns represented the norm, not Edward's.[1]

But as a Catholic administration was inaugurated, so too was greater control over the printers and stationers of Mary's England. Before the new queen had even arrived in London, after the tense standoff with her Protestant rival, Lady Jane Grey (1537–1554), a new agenda had already been set in motion. By the end of July 1553, with Mary's reign less than a month old, the Privy Council issued a new proclamation, from the press of John Cawood (1514–1572), the queen's new printer, suppressing the printing of seditious rumors. Cawood had replaced Richard Grafton, who had printed a proclamation naming Jane Grey the new queen and had also intemperately signed his name to it with the words "Reginæ a typographia excusum," implying royal sanction. That the royal privilege was the only thing he lost is perhaps a minor miracle in itself. As part of her coronation ceremonies, Mary issued a general pardon, but it did not extend to Grafton or his collaborator in the printing of the Great Bible, Edward Whitchurch (d. 1561). Their unpardonable crime was that they had issued Henry's authorized version of the English Bible as well as *The Book of Common Prayer* and collections of Protestant homilies. What they had legally printed only a year before was now used as evidence of their heresy and sedition.

1. Blayney, *Stationers' Company*, 604–6.

One of the most interesting cases of survival during Mary's reign was that of the printer John Day. He and his business partner, William Seres (d. ca. 1579), were among the "godly men" who had operated a press in London during the days of the boy king.[2] Although Day disappeared after the return of Catholic rule in England, he was far from inactive. Unlike Grafton, whose shop, type, and ornaments were taken over by the Catholic printer Robert Caly (the only Catholic printer to have gone into exile during Edward's reign), Day simply closed his shop in Aldersgate and probably took some of his type with him. For while no texts appear with his own imprint between July or August of 1553 and 1556, the evidence of type very strongly suggests that he continued to print Protestant works clandestinely under the name of Michael Wood, with some indication that he operated his shop on the property of Sir William Cecil, who would play a key role during Elizabeth's reign.

---

2. Evenden, *Patents and Patronage*, 30.

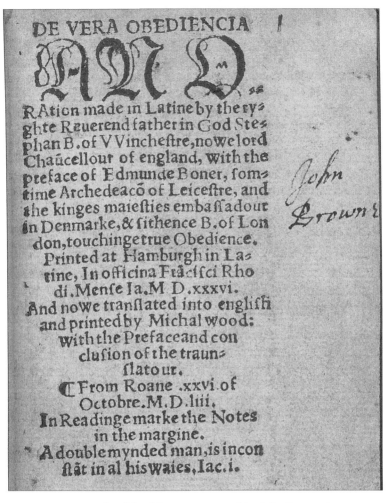

An example of the false imprint used by John Day under
the pseudonym Michael Wood.

Some twelve books and ten pamphlets appear under
Michael Wood's false imprint using Day's type, the
last one appearing some five months before Day was

arrested in Norfolk on 16 October 1554.[3] He may have been apprehended for illicit printing or perhaps for smuggling contraband literature. It is also possible, however, that he was arrested after something as ordinary as receiving a consignment of a large amount of paper. Its arrival from the Continent would have alerted local authorities to the fact that a press was in operation, which would then rouse curiosity as to whether it was a legal or an illegal one. Given that Day had not apparently printed anything since the previous May, it is likely that he ran out of that most basic of supplies and, through the purchase, led a trail straight to his hidden-workshop door.[4] Whatever the reason, Day found himself imprisoned in the Tower, where he met the Bible translator John Rogers (d. 1555), who encouraged him to remain faithful to the Protestant cause in such trying times. Rogers would become the first person to be executed as a religious dissenter under Queen Mary.

Day's release from prison is just as mysterious as his original arrest. As an expert printer, especially of psalters, it has been suggested that Day's skills were needed for the printing of the new Catholic primers that Mary's court wanted to see reintroduced in order to replace the Protestant ones that had appeared under her predecessors Henry and Edward.[5] Whatever the reason, Day resumed printing in 1556, but as the assign of the Catholic printer John Wayland (d. 1571),

3. Blayney, *Stationers' Company*, 804–7.
4. Evenden and Freeman, *Religion*, 37.
5. Evenden and Freeman, *Religion*, 42.

a task that meant not only working under his supervision but doing so in full awareness that Wayland was a spy who served as an informer to Mary's agents. Wayland had been granted the patent for printing primers and devotional works early in Mary's reign, meaning that Day was now assembling type for the very Catholic texts he had promised Rogers he would fight against. Day's survival, however, both as a printer and as a living, breathing human being, were dependent on carrying out these duties without protest, and the typographical evidence indicates that he did so. Ironically for the man who in 1548 had printed *John Bon and the Mast Person*, ridiculing the Catholic doctrine of the Eucharist, Day was now responsible for printing treatises in defense of the doctrine of transubstantiation. It was a confusing time indeed. John Day's name appears on the original charter of the Company of Stationers, drafted upon the Company's establishment in May of 1557. John Wayland's name, however, does not, owing to the fact that he was a scrivener and not a freeman of the Stationers' Company.

So, certainly this was a time of confusion for Protestant printers and stationers during the brief reign of Mary I. It also appears to have been a confusing era for the Marian court as well, as it had the difficult task of determining which religious materials were suitable for printing and which were not. They must have realized that, in the end, while religious practice could be legislated and enforced, actual belief could not. Theirs were indeed very uncertain times. The Christian faithful of England had embraced neither the theology nor practice found in the Reformed churches of Geneva or Zurich, nor was there undiluted support for the old ways of the Church of Rome. Although the Catholic party had full control of the religious agenda and papal jurisdiction was being re-imposed, the printing projects they sponsored bore very little resemblance to the efforts of the Catholic Reformation on the Continent. What were missing from the English scene at this time were the great Catholic Reformation authors and texts that abounded in France, Italy, and Spain. No Ignatius of Loyola, no John of the Cross was printed in England. And just as the forces of the Catholic Reformation were beginning to work toward greater centralization and standardization across the Catholic world, under Mary, English Catholic printing was looking more insular. The vast majority of religious books printed during her reign were devotional or liturgical, and they harkened back to the church's medieval glory days. For example, some thirty-five editions of the Sarum Rite primers—that is, Catholic prayer books based on local, ancient English rites—were printed.[6]

6. Evenden and Freeman, *Religion*, 41.

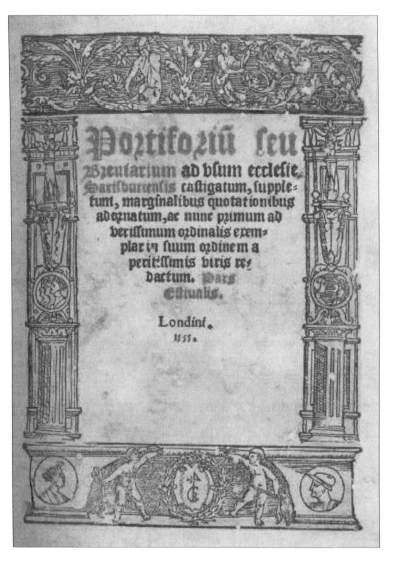

Title page to the Sarum Rite breviary *Portiforium seu Breviarium ad usum ecclesie Sarisburiensis*, printed at London in 1555.

And yet, the most popular Catholic books of Henry VIII's reign, such as *The Golden Legend* and St. Brigid's fifteen *Oes*, were not reprinted during this time at all. There was little stomach for the publication of controversial material. Mary and her restored Catholic episcopate likely realized that nostalgia for late English Catholicism could not restore it, but they were clearly uncertain about how to proceed. Had Mary and her archbishop of Canterbury, Reginald Cardinal Pole (1500–1558), lived longer, a clearer Catholic vision of the religious future might have emerged, a vision that would have both shaped and been shaped by the local print trade.

6

Renewal under Elizabeth

WHEN ELIZABETH I (1533–1603) succeeded in 1558, the pendulum swung once again back toward the Protestant camp. In less than twenty-five years, the English faithful had bounced back and forth between Catholic and Reformed theology and practice, tied almost exclusively to the religious sensibilities of whichever Tudor monarch had then sat on the throne. Elizabeth would pursue a *via media*, history says, but this new shift would largely translate into good news for those who believed in the cause of reform and bad news for those whose loyalties to the old Roman Church had been rewarded under her late half-sister Mary. It was no different for the printers. Among those who benefited from this change in regime was Richard Grafton, who once again emerged from the shadows, taking possession of the types and ornaments he had surrendered to Robert Caly and had used during Mary's reign to print Catholic books at his own press. The erstwhile Catholic Caly, who had smuggled Catholic books into England during Edward's reign, understood which way the winds were definitively blowing this time. He was among the first to take advantage of Elizabeth's coronation pardon in January of 1559. John Day would, of course, be another winner in this struggle.

In collaboration with John Foxe (1516–1587), he would produce the *Actes and Monuments*, without doubt the definitive Elizabethan account of the persecution of English Protestants by the Roman Church.

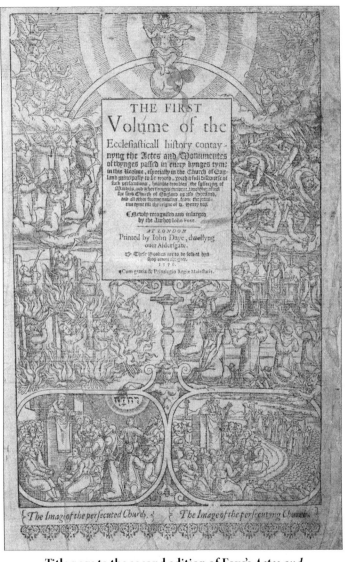

Title page to the second edition of Foxe's *Actes and Monuments*, printed by John Day at London in 1570.

Memorialized within this exhaustive two-million-word narrative, more commonly known as Foxe's *Book of Martyrs*, are the sufferings of the various Reformers, here cleverly and closely associated with the persecution of primitive Christian saints as described in the book of Revelation and early martyrologies. Foxe and Day depict a vivid pageant of oppressed souls stretching back in time to the Roman emperors, with their focus, however, firmly trained on the pope and his minions as heirs to those early pagan tormentors. As one scholar describes it, "in Foxe's writings the papacy and Catholicism were, and had been from time immemorial, the perpetual enemy. The war between the persecuted church of God and the synagogue of Satan had been waged since the world began, but had climaxed in the sixteenth century, with the rise of Luther and the open confrontation between the true and the false Churches."[1] Foxe's *Book of Martyrs* helped to entrench the myth of a divinely ordained Protestant England in the British consciousness that lasted well into the twentieth century. Among its detailed accounts may, of course, be found eyewitness reports of the executions of Cranmer, Hugh Latimer (ca. 1487-1555), and Nicholas Ridley (ca. 1500-1555).

Foxe himself was well placed to write and promote his magnum opus. A fellow of Magdalen College, Oxford, he served as tutor to Thomas Howard, later the fourth duke of Norfolk, in the mid-1540s before fleeing his homeland with the accession of Queen Mary. On the Continent he found work with

1. *Duffy, Saints*, 35.

the Protestant printer Joannes Oporinus (1507–1568) in Basel and was exposed to likeminded evangelicals who influenced his thought and encouraged his writing. After returning to England he found favor with Queen Elizabeth's secretary of state, William Cecil (1520–1598), who effectively sponsored the massive work. Foxe's activities with Oporinus had prepared him well for collaboration with Day, who was considered one of the most innovative of the printers of the new Elizabethan age.

When first issued, Foxe's *Martyrs* was among the largest publishing endeavors ever undertaken in Britain. It occupied all of Day's presses for eighteen months to the exclusion of every other project, with Day himself borrowing five hundred pounds to cover the cost of paper alone.[2] Foxe's interventions during the printing process are evident by the number of cancels and slipcancels to be found in all of the editions printed during his lifetime, creating nightmare scenarios for bibliographers.[3] The text grew dramatically in size and weight after the publication of the already lengthy 1563 first English edition as the author responded to the charges of egregious error, some quite justifiably leveled against him by Catholic apologists such as Nicholas Sanders (d. 1581). Nevertheless, with the inclusion of official documents (some of which Day may have already secretly printed during

2. Freeman and Greengrass, "The Making of Martyrs."

3. Roberts, "Bibliographical Aspects," 44–48. A "cancel" is a leaf inserted into a book, replacing one containing errors. A "slipcancel" is a smaller piece of paper pasted over part of the text on a page.

Mary's reign[4]), eyewitness testimonies, and revision of its faults, Foxe and Day cemented the book's reputation as genuine history, and the air of authority that it enjoyed in its early days was only reinforced by the fact that large sections of it were subsumed into the 1577 edition of Holinshed's *Chronicles*. Together with Shakespeare and the Bible, it is one of the very few books never out of print in England before 1900. Not surprisingly, it had a very limited readership in Catholic Europe, a fact that only served to bolster the domestic perception of Britain as an island refuge blessed by divine providence and shielded from the self-evident errors of Rome. Foxe's determination to dwell on the outrages committed specifically against Protestants in England and Scotland, on the other hand, helped to emphasize the obviously divine favor for the cause of godly reform in the British Isles.[5]

4. King, "John Day", p. 206.
5. Heal, "Appropriating History," 117.

Woodcut illustration of the burning of Simon Myller and Elizabeth Cooper from the first edition Foxe's *Actes and Monuments*, London, 1563.

The early editions of Foxe, printed by Day, are perhaps best remembered for their iconography. Woodcut images of torture and death, with diabolical-looking friars and patriarchal-looking martyrs, added to the controversial nature of the book and were intended to elicit an emotional and empathetic response from the viewer, especially those who were unable to read the text itself.

Woodcut illustration of Edmund Bonner, bishop of London, beating a Protestant, from the first edition Foxe's *Actes and Monuments*, London, 1563.

In spite of the Calvinist injunction against imagery, it was not unusual to find the woodcuts sold separately and hung in family homes; and despite the expense (roughly twenty-four shillings per bound volume[6]), a copy of the book was placed in every cathedral in England. Its appearance among the bequests of ordinary citizens underlines its centrality to

6. Roberts, "Bibliographical Aspects," 48.

seventeenth-century Protestant piety.[7] So popular were the various editions of the book that Foxe referred to John Day's press as "our printing treadmill."[8] Day, one of the "godly men" from the reign of Edward VI, having survived Mary's administration, was seen by Foxe as "one of the instruments of true religion, sent to repair Christ's church."[9] Godly indeed, but also very wealthy, thanks to Foxe and the three-hundred fifty other titles Day issued in the course of his career. He was also a man who understood the value in business of monopoly, which he obtained for several titles during Elizabeth's reign. By the time of his death, Day's wealth was estimated at five thousand pounds.

7. Watt, *Cheap Print*, 158.
8. King, "Light," 55.
9. King, "Light," 67.

Portrait of John Day, used as a printer's device in 1564.

7

Catholic Printers
under Elizabeth

THOSE AUTHORS AND PRINTERS who remained
loyal to the old church were caught in a strange vise
that emerged during the Elizabethan period. On the
one hand, especially at the beginning of the reign,
there was a growing desire for religious tolerance,
expressed by the queen herself, who professed to
have no desire to see into men's souls. On the other
hand, especially after her excommunication by Pope
Pius V (1504–1572) in 1570, the attempted assaults
on the queen's person by Catholics like Sir Anthony
Babington, and the Spanish invasion threat of 1588,
there was a greater clamor for the control of seditious and heretical writings. The odd result was that
Catholics were free to believe but not to worship and
that printers who, by their books and pamphlets, as-
sisted and brought comfort to Catholics could be arrested and tried for sedition rather than heresy.

Catholic printers were forced to go into hiding
once again. It is known that three clandestine Catholic

presses operated in London between the years 1578 and 1582, for example, in the years before the Spanish Armada. William Carter (d. 1584) ran a press on Tower Hill, Richard Rowland (d. 1640) operated another in Smithfield, and Stephen Brinkley (fl. 1585) manned the third, in East Ham. Each of the presses was eventually discovered and dismantled. Carter, who had apprenticed under the Queen's Printer John Cawood during the reign of Queen Mary, was executed for printing Father Gregory Martin's *A Treatise of Schism*, which had been deemed treasonous. Rowland, however, fled to the Continent, where he produced polemical works under the name of Richard Verstegan. His most famous and influential was his *Theatrum crudelitatum haereticorum temporis nostrae*, published at Antwerp in 1588, the year of the Armada.

Title page to Verstegan's visual polemic against the
persecution of Catholics by Protestants, printed at
Antwerp in the Armada year, 1588.

Unlike some other Catholic publications of the period, this book was not intended to inspire the faithful to martyrdom so much as rouse in them a sense of indignant horror at Protestant atrocities. The book was designed in four distinct parts by Verstegan so that they could be sold separately if so desired.[1] The first part deals with the persecution of Catholics under Henry VIII; the second, the persecution by the Huguenots during the first civil war in France in 1562; the third, the persecution by Calvinist soldiers under William of Orange against Flemish Catholics; and the last, the abuse of Irish and English Catholics under Elizabeth I. By far, the most violent illustrations appear in parts two and three, and while the images are self-explanatory, each also has a six-line hexameter verse composed by Johannes Bochius, town secretary of Antwerp, reflecting on the sorrowful scene displayed. For example, beneath the only known contemporaneous image of the execution of Margaret Clitherow, the York martyr, he writes, "Female sex, your reputation commends you also. The stout heroine was not dejected even in the midst of extreme torture. The weights and millstones did not disquiet your tender body. No, she said, 'Place mountains upon my limbs. My innocent spirit shall pass through the ruins of my body and reach the stars.'" Each engraving includes a legend with letters corresponding to a description on the facing page that editorializes as well as explains the scene.

1. Dillon, *Construction*, 244.

Perfecutiones aduerfus Catholicos à Prote-
ftantibus Caluiniftis excitæ in Anglia.

Et tua femineum commendat gloria fexum,
Dura nec in fummis animo demiffa virago
Suppliciis, teneràmque tui non pondera molem
Corporis, iniecti non turbauere molares:
Quin, ait, his totos membris imponite montes,
Spiritus innocua tranfcendet ad aftra ruina.

K 3   Pres-

The martyrdom of Margaret Clitherow of York from
Verstegan's *Theatrum*.

Verstegan purposely called his work a "theatre," since, as he explained, "the eye is held by pictures, and what is brought before the eyes has greater effect than that which is brought to the ears." The intentionally repugnant character of the illustrations combined with their poetic reflections to serve as a "thinly disguised political and military manifesto for Philip II," who governed Flanders at this time.[2] Verstegan established himself at Antwerp in 1587, only two years after the city had been reclaimed from the Calvinists by Spanish Catholic forces. In that same year he published the first edition of this book, shortly after the execution of Mary, Queen of Scots, whom he declared the legitimate heir to the English crown. Not surprisingly, the tableau of her death features last in the *Theatrum*. The work, which saw eight editions in twenty-two years and inspired contemporaneous Continental Catholic propagandists such as Michael ab Isselt (d. 1597) and Lawrence Beyerlinck (1578–1627), has been described by some scholars as an Armada pamphlet. By means of it Verstegan was helping to provide Catholic Europe with a justification for the invasion of England in response to the sufferings of the English Catholics depicted herein. The unsuccessful invasion was, of course, attempted in the year that this edition appeared.

Among the Catholic printers, the case of Stephen Brinkley is in many ways the most interesting. His press was a typically small operation, set up in the private home of Francis Browne, the brother of the

2. Dillon, *Construction*, 275.

Viscount Montague, in East Ham, where he hoped to avoid the suspicions of local authorities.[3] The Jesuit Father Robert Persons (1546–1610), one of the priests who worked for the reconversion of England during Elizabeth's reign, recorded that seven men continually worked Brinkley's East Ham press day and night, issuing pamphlets and small books to counter the steady stream of propaganda being published by the licensed Protestant press. Persons was arguably the most adept at harnessing the power of the illegal Catholic press. A Somerset recusant, he had returned to England in 1580 as one of the first Jesuit missionaries committed to the reconversion of the island. While his confrère Edmund Campion (1540–1581) attempted to arouse enthusiasm for the old religion through his homiletical skills, Persons worked at sowing the seeds of political discontent through his publications.[4] At East Ham, Brinkley published at least six books bearing a false Louvain imprint before one of his servants was arrested and racked until he revealed the location of the press, which was subsequently destroyed. Undeterred, Persons then moved his theater of operations to Stonor Park, about twenty miles from London, where two more books were printed before Brinkley was arrested and tortured in the Tower of London in August of 1581.[5] Realizing that their mission was seriously compromised, Persons abandoned Britain about this time and never

3. Loades, *Politics*, 120.

4. Klein, *Intolerance*, 40.

5. Houliston, *Catholic Resistance*, 34.

45

saw his homeland again. The Jesuit fled for Rouen, France, explaining that one of his principal reasons for leaving at that time was "to set up some sort of printing press in some place nearby where the books could be printed which are brought out by our fathers in English as circumstances call for them."[6] Besides Rouen, Persons would eventually keep the presses of Paris, Douai, and Louvain all busy in service to his cause.

The conditions in which Brinkley and his confrères operated before his arrest are most interesting. Unlike their Protestant counterparts, Catholic printers generally worked in cramped domestic settings (rather than in shops) with old, creaking presses that constantly threatened to betray their activities to their neighbors as well as to the watch patrolling the streets outside.[7] Brinkley was understandably cautious. Printing, of course, is a filthy business, the blackest of the arts, but he insisted that his workers should always appear in public dressed in the finest, cleanest linens, with not a single mark on their hands, riding the most impressive horses, all to avoid unwanted attention. And while the local vicar and wardens noticed that the men did not attend Anglican services, it was not their non-attendance at church that led to their capture. In the end, as may have happened with John Day in Mary's reign, it was their injudicious purchase of a large amount of paper that gave rise to suspicions

6. Robert Persons, S.J., to Alphonsus Agazzari, S.J., 21 October 1581, in Persons, *Christian Directory*, xxxix.

7. Childs, *God's Traitors*, 66.

that a secret press was in operation in the parish.[8] Amazingly, Brinkley escaped and made his way to Rome, as did other English Catholic printers. When operations in England became too dangerous, small presses were regularly packed up by Catholic exiles and moved to the Continent, to places like Douai, Saint-Omer, and Valladolid. The dangers associated with the production of these Catholic books and their subsequent smuggling back into England cannot be overestimated. It was not only the *printing* of a Catholic text that was a capital offence warranting the punishment of being hung, drawn, and quartered; so was the mere possession of a book that had been issued by a Catholic press. This situation would not significantly change until the late seventeenth century.

The Venerable English College at Rome, among the most important seminaries training men for the reconversion of England, was also a center of recusant Catholic publication. One of the finest examples of Catholic Reformation propaganda issued by the College is the *Ecclesiæ anglicanæ trophaea*, the great book of engravings done by Giovanni Battista Cavalieri (1595–1597) after paintings by Nicolò Circignano (1520?–1596?) and hastily printed by Bartolomeo Grassi in 1584.

8. Evenden and Freeman, *Religion*, 29.

Title page to the *Ecclesiæ anglicanæ trophaea*,
published by the Catholic priests of the
Venerable Roman College in 1584.

Two churches in Catholic Reformation Rome are particularly associated with Circignano: San Stefano Rotondo (once part of the German-Hungarian College) and the English College Chapel, both of which featured his gruesome frescoes. The graphic depictions of the torments and deaths of Christian martyrs from the first to the sixteenth centuries were intended to inspire seminarians returning to their home countries to face persecution at the hands of Protestants with the same zeal as those who had gone before them. This catalogue of Circignano's thirty-four frescoes, engraved by Cavalieri, records the cycle of death and spiritual triumph devised by the artist as it originally appeared on the walls of the college. The first twenty-four panels depict martyrs up to the reign of Henry VIII, with the last ten devoted to those who died during the English Reformation itself. The last painting depicts the death of Richard Thirkeld, who was executed at York in May of 1583, meaning that Circignano "was working in the manner of a war artist who recorded in these final scenes the reports received from the battlefield."[9] The book was published by the priests of the College in June of 1584, less than a year after the chapel decoration was completed, in order to extend the propaganda value of the paintings beyond the college precincts.[10] The frescoes were lost when the chapel was destroyed at the end of the eighteenth century, making this volume all the more important, since it was used to reproduce the

9. Dillon, *Construction*, 176–77.
10. Witcombe, *Copyright*, 165.

series when the adornment of the new chapel was completed in 1893.[11]

The artist's imagery is cleverly and deliberately provocative. The saints' executioners are generally depicted in the dress of ancient Roman centurions, thereby linking the martyrs' sufferings with those who first gave their blood for the life of the church. At the same time, those being martyred and the watching crowd are shown in Tudor dress, making it abundantly clear that these horrors were occurring right there and then. They can only be fully appreciated against the backdrop of the Herculean struggle between representatives of the English Catholic Church and the Church of England, with each professing to be the true heirs of the apostolic community in Britain stretching back in time to the legend of Joseph of Arimathea. Cavalieri's book would never be popular in England, of course, but that was immaterial by this point because the provocative illustrations were intended to do much more than merely inspire Catholic divinity students. They were now designed to inspire outrage on the Continent and encourage a military invasion of England, such as would occur four years later with the Spanish Armada.[12]

11. Dillon, *Construction*, 192.

12. Walsham, "Domme Preachers," 99–100.

8

Conclusion

A BRIEF SURVEY LIKE this does little more than highlight what most students of this tumultuous era already appreciate: that whatever romantic notions popular culture may attach to the Tudor period, most would not have wanted to live through the reality of it. What made the confusion of English printers different from that of most of their fellow citizens, even touching them with dread at times, was this: they could not deny their association with the product of their labors. The names proudly displayed at the bottom of the title page of the Great Bible in 1539, for example, would stand as evidence against these printers by the end of Henry's reign. Even if their names were not visible for all to see in every case, the type and ornaments they owned and used bore witness to them and their deeds. While some printers may have changed their religious principles depending on which way the royal wind blew, others must have looked at their confusing situation and realized that they were being undone by the very invention by which they had brought revolution to England in the first place.

So what did this confusion of printers eventually lead to? The whiplash effect from the reigns of the four Tudor monarchs caused printers and publishers to begin to sense that freedom of expression in religious matters was perhaps preferable to the whims of monarchs. Their collective experience, whether as Catholic, Anglican, or Puritan printers, was that the English Reformation was not simply about personal choices. It had also been about coercion and compulsion, and for those who practiced this trade, sometimes that meant keeping their heads down and plowing through while waiting for better days. What the authors and printers and booksellers were on the forefront of discovering, whether consciously or subconsciously, was that life's most important questions could have divergent, incompatible answers. Their job was to put those incompatible answers into the public arena. This recognition, born out of confusion, was ultimately moving the English-speaking world toward the acknowledgement of the value, if not yet the right, of free expression. It was certainly by no means won by the end of Elizabeth's reign. But it helped to set the stage for the struggle to achieve the freedom of the press, which would begin with the lapse of the Licensing Act in 1695 and continues to this day around the globe. But it was the Puritan John Milton (1608–1674) who would provide the philosophical underpinning for that freedom when in 1644 he would write in his *Areopagitica* the following words: "Books are not absolutely dead things, but doe contain a potencie of life in them to be as active as that soule was whose progeny they are; nay they do preserve as in a violl the purest efficacie and extraction of that living intellect that bred them" and went on to declare "Give me the liberty to know, to utter, and to argue freely according to conscience, above all liberties."[1] That precious liberty, which would be valued above almost all others in the English-speaking world, however, was born from a confusion of printers.

1. Milton, *Areopagitica*, 4, 35.

Bibliography

Blayney, Peter W. M. *The Stationers' Company and the Printers of London 1501–1557*. Cambridge: Cambridge University Press, 2013.

Childs, Jessie. *God's Traitors: Terror and Faith in Elizabethan England*. London: Bodley Head, 2014.

Daniell, David. *William Tyndale: A Biography*. New Haven: Yale University Press, 2001.

Dillon, Anne. *The Construction of Martyrdom in the English Catholic Community, 1535–1603*. Aldershot, UK: Ashgate, 2002.

Duffy, Eamon. *Saints, Sacrilege and Sedition: Religion and Conflict in the Tudor Reformations* London: Bloomsbury, 2012.

Evenden, Elizabeth, and Thomas Freeman. *Religion and the Book in Early Modern England*. Cambridge: Cambridge University Press, 2011.

———. *Patents and Patronage: The Life and Career of John Day, Tudor Printer*. PhD thesis, University of York, 2002. http://etheses. whiterose.ac.uk/id/eprint/2455.

Freeman, Thomas, and Mark Greengrass. "The Making of Martyrs." *BBC History Magazine*, February 2012. https://www.historyextra. com/magazine-issue/february-2012.

Gilmont, J.-F. *The Reformation and the Book*. Aldershot, UK: Ashgate, 1998.

Heal, Felicity. "Appropriating History: Catholic and Protestant Polemics and the National Past." *The Huntington Library Quarterly* (2005) 109–32.

Herbert, A. S. *Historical Catalogue of Printed Editions of the English Bible 1525–1961*. London: British and Foreign Bible Society, 1968.

Houliston, Victor. *Catholic Resistance in Elizabethan England: Robert Persons's Jesuit Polemic, 1580–1610.* Aldershot, UK: Ashgate, 2007.

Killick, Helen. "Treason, Felony, and Lollardy." *Historical Research* 89 (2016) 227–45.

King, John N. "John Day: Master Printer of the English Reformation." In *The Beginnings of English Protestantism*, edited by Peter Marshall, 180–208. Cambridge: Cambridge University Press, 2002.

————. "'The Light of Printing': William Tyndale, John Foxe, John Day, and Early Modern Print Culture." *Renaissance Quarterly* (2001) 52–85.

Klein, A. J. *Intolerance in the Reign of Elizabeth, Queen of England.* Port Washington, NY: Kennikat, 1917.

Lewis, Jack P. *The English Bible from KJV to NIV: A History and Evaluation.* Grand Rapids: Baker, 1991.

Loades, David. *Politics, Censorship and the English Reformation.* London: Pinter, 1991.

Marshall, Peter. *Heretics and Believers.* New Haven: Yale University Press, 2017.

Milton, John. *Areopagtica.* London: n.p., 1644.

The Newe Testament Dylygently Corrected and Compared with the Greke. Antwerp: Emperowr, 1534.

Pardue, Brad C. *Printing, Power, and Piety.* Leiden: Brill, 2012.

Persons, Robert. *The Christian Directory.* Edited by Victor Houliston. Leiden: Brill, 1998.

Roberts, Julian. "Bibliographical Aspects: John Foxe." In *Foxe and the English Reformation*, edited by David Loades, 44–48. Aldershot: Scolar, 1997.

Walsham, Alexandra. "'Domme Preachers'? Post-Reformation English Catholicism and the Culture of Print." *Past & Present* 168 (2000) 72–123.

Watt, Tessa. *Cheap Print and Popular Piety, 1550–1640.* Cambridge: Cambridge University Press, 1991.

Witcombe, Christopher L. C. E. *Copyright in the Renaissance.* Leiden: Brill, 2004.